GERMANY

Cath Senker

Photographs by Christof Schürpf

CHERRYTREE BOOKS

LETTERS FROM
AROUND THE WORLD

Distributed in the United States by
Cherrytree Books
1980 Lookout Drive
North Mankato, MN 56001

Library of Congress Cataloging-in-Publication Data applied
for.

First Edition
9 8 7 6 5 4 3 2 1

First published in 2005 by
Evans Brothers Ltd
2A Portman Mansions
Chiltern Street
London W1U 6NR

Conceived and produced by

Nutshell
MEDIA

www.nutshellmedialtd.co.uk

Editor: Polly Goodman
Design: Mayer Media Ltd
Cartography: Encompass Graphics Ltd
Artwork: Mayer Media Ltd
Consultants: Jeff Stanfield and Anne Spiring

All photographs were taken by Christof Schürpf.

Printed in China.

Acknowledgments
The photographer would like to thank the Böhm family,
the staff and students of Turnseeschule, Freiburg,
Staatsweingut Blankenhornsberg, the University of
Freiburg, and the Islamic Center of Freiburg for all
their help with this book.

Cover: Paul and two of his neighbors, Anna and Lukas,
standing in front of the Münster cathedral, the most
famous building in Freiburg.
Title page: Paul and his friends, Julius and Benjamin, in
their soccer club uniforms on the field near Paul's home.
This page: A vineyard near Ihringen, about 15 miles
(25 km) from Freiburg.
Contents page: Paul in summer clothes.
Glossary page: Paul on his bike with his sister Carla.
Further Information page: Paul with his friends in the
soccer team.
Index: The German flag flying from a boat on the Rhine.

Contents

My Country

Saturday, September 25

Scheffelstrasse 84
3rd floor
71903 Freiburg
Germany

Dear Kerry,

Hallo! (In German, this means the same as it does in English.)

My name is Paul Böhm (pronounced "Powl Berm"). I'm eight years old and I live in Freiburg im Breisgau (pronounced "Fry-borg im Brize-gow"), a city in Breisgau, in southwest Germany. I live with my mom, dad, and my sister Carla, who's 14.

I'm learning English, so it's great to practice with a real English speaker!

Write back soon!

From
Paul

Here I am in the back garden with my mom, Gabi, my dad, Thomas, and Carla. →

Germany is in Western Europe. In 1945, after World War II, it was divided into two: East Germany and West Germany. In 1990, the country became one again.

Germany's place in the world.

DENMARK

North Sea

Baltic Sea

N

Hamburg

Bremen

Elbe

Weser

POLAND

BERLIN

NETHERLANDS

GERMANY

Elbe

Essen

Leipzig

Dresden

Cologne

Rhine

BELGIUM

CZECH REPUBLIC

Frankfurt am Main

LUX.

Danube

FRANCE

Rhine

Stuttgart

BLACK FOREST

Danube

Munich

VOSGES

Freiburg im Breisgau

Lake Constance

BAVARIAN ALPS

AUSTRIA

SWITZERLAND

△ Zugspitze 9,715 ft (2,962 m)

Germany shares borders with nine countries and has coastlines with two seas, the Baltic Sea and the North Sea.

5

Freiburg im Breisgau (Freiburg for short) is close to the borders of France and Switzerland. It is an important center for trade in timber (wood) and wine. Goods can be brought in and sent to other countries by highway (the *Autobahn*), rail, and air.

Freiburg is an eco-city, which means people try to protect the environment. Some industries run on solar power. Others make solar products, such as solar panels to heat water.

A view over Freiburg, with the Vosges mountains in France in the distance. Most of the city was rebuilt after it was bombed in World War II, so there are many modern buildings.

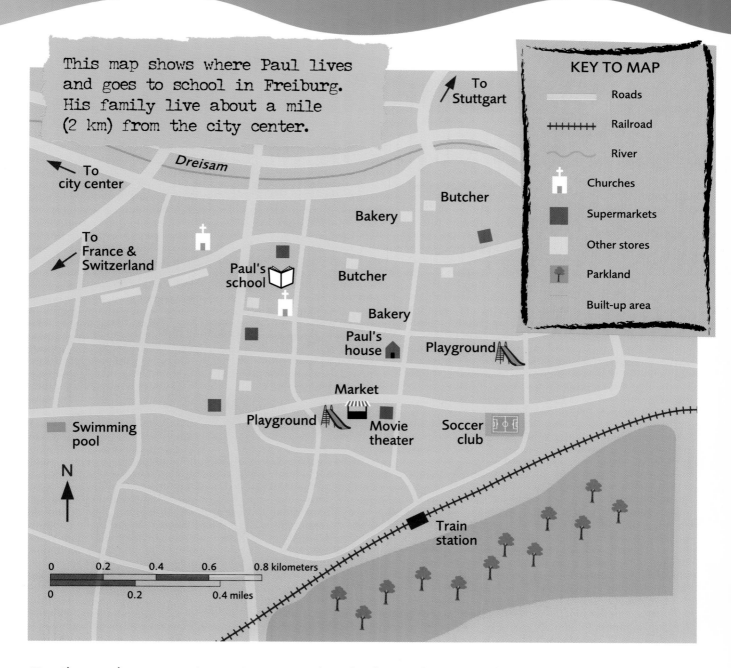

This map shows where Paul lives and goes to school in Freiburg. His family live about a mile (2 km) from the city center.

KEY TO MAP

Roads	
Railroad	
River	
Churches	
Supermarkets	
Other stores	
Parkland	
Built-up area	

To Stuttgart

Dreisam

To city center

To France & Switzerland

Butcher

Bakery

Paul's school

Butcher

Bakery

Paul's house

Playground

Market

Swimming pool

Playground

Movie theater

Soccer club

N

Train station

0   0.2   0.4   0.6   0.8 kilometers
0   0.2   0.4 miles

Freiburg has a university, a cathedral, and several other interesting historical buildings. Many tourists visit the city and businesses hold conferences there.

The Dreisam river runs through the city on its way to the Rhine, Germany's main river. The Rhine is about 9 miles (15 km) away from Freiburg.

Landscape and Weather

Freiburg is near the Black Forest, a mountain region covered in forests. Farther east there are high mountains, called the Bavarian Alps. In the north there are low, flat plains.

It rarely gets very hot or very cold in Germany. Winters are mild in the north, where the land is low. In the high Bavarian Alps, the winters are colder and it often snows.

The Rhine river begins in Switzerland. It runs through Germany and the Netherlands, before reaching the North Sea.

Freiburg's Climate

January

Temperature
39 °F
(4 °C)

Rainfall
2.5 in
(61 mm)

July

Temperature
75 °F
(24 °C)

Rainfall
4 in
(106 mm)

At Home

Like many people living in Germany's cities, Paul and his family live in an apartment. It is on the top floor of a large house. There are three other apartments in the house, one on each floor.

Paul and Carla in front of their house. They play here in their neighbors' back yard with friends.

Family members watch TV, listen to the stereo, and read in the living room.

Paul has lots of toy cars and trucks, and his own CD player.

In the apartment there are three bedrooms, a living room, kitchen, and bathroom. There is a large hallway where the family keeps the piano.

Paul's bedroom has a high bed with a special slide so he can get up quickly in the morning! Paul has a desk in his room where he does his homework.

Paul brushes his teeth every morning and evening with his electric toothbrush.

Paul's apartment has two balconies. They are used for hanging out laundry, growing plants, or for sitting in the sunshine. There is a back yard, too, which is shared with people in the other apartments.

Paul is watering the plants on the balcony. Freiburg gets plenty of sunshine, so it's easy to grow flowers.

Saturday, October 23

Scheffelstrasse 84
3rd floor
71903 Freiburg
Germany

Hallo Kerry,

Wie geht's? (You say "Vee-gates." That's German for "How are you?")

Thanks for your letter. I've got a pet rabbit, too. His name's Ronja. I give him hay to eat and brush his fur to keep him clean. Ronja's hutch is in the back yard and every week I clean it out. I let him run around in the yard but I can't leave him out in case he eats the plants. It's important to take care of the yard because we share it with the people in the other apartments.

Bye for now

From

Paul

Here I am with Ronja in the back garden.

Food and Mealtimes

Most mornings, Paul has a bowl of granola for breakfast, followed by a roll with butter and jam. Sometimes he has a boiled egg.

On weekends, the family usually eats breakfast together. On weekdays, they help themselves to breakfast as soon as they get up. Paul's dad has usually eaten his breakfast and left for work by the time Paul gets up.

Paul and Carla have an egg, cereal, and rolls for breakfast. German adults and older children usually drink coffee with their breakfast.

On summer weekends, the family barbecues sausages and eat their meals in the back yard.

Carla and Paul have lunch with their mother at home. They usually eat a small lunch of pasta and salad.

The family eats dinner together between 6 and 8 p.m. They usually have noodles, pasta, or a rice dish with vegetables or salad. Most German people have meat with their main meal, but Paul's family doesn't have meat every day.

Paul's mom prepares a salad with fresh basil grown on the balcony.

Paul's family walks to the local butcher's and bakery for fresh meat and bread, and buy fruit and vegetables at the outdoor market. Gabi grows herbs on one of the balconies, and tomatoes in the garden. She drives to the supermarket for the main shopping.

Friday, November 19

Scheffelstrasse 84
3rd floor
71903 Freiburg
Germany.

Hi Kerry,

Here's a recipe for *kartoffelpuffer*, or potato pancakes:

You will need: 6 medium potatoes, peeled and grated; 1 onion, grated; 2 eggs; $\frac{1}{2}$ teaspoon salt; pepper; 4 tablespoons flour; 1 teaspoon parsley; 2 tablespoons cooking oil.

1. Mix the potatoes with the eggs, flour, onion, parsley, salt, and pepper.
2. Heat the oil in a frying pan and add 3 tablespoons of the mixture. This will make one pancake.
3. Spread the mixture evenly and fry on both sides until golden brown. Now make the other pancakes in the same way.

Guten Appetit! (This means "Enjoy your food!")

Paul

Here are the potato pancakes I made with my mom. We ate them with apple sauce — delicious! →

School Day

Every school morning, Paul leaves the house at 8:30 a.m. It takes him 10 minutes to walk to school, which is close to home.

Lessons start at 8:40 a.m and finish at 1 p.m. At 10:15 a.m there is a half-hour recess, when the children can play games in the playground.

Paul started school when he was 6 years old. When he is 10, he will go to the secondary school next door.

Paul arrives at school with his friend Luca. As in most German schools, there is no uniform.

Paul studies geography, German, math, religious education, art, and sports. The teachers use games to make sure that learning is fun.

There are two school terms a year in Germany, from September to February, and from February to July. The main vacations are the six-week summer vacation and two weeks at Christmas.

Every hour, Paul's class has a five-minute recess and a stretch to keep the pupils fresh for their classes.

Paul's class is making an ocean display in the art lesson. Paul cuts out a fish he has drawn to add it to the display.

Even though Paul only goes to school in the morning, he does lots of activities after school. He is a member of a soccer club that practices once a week after school. Every Monday afternoon he has a piano lesson.

Paul jumps over the boxes in gym.

Paul has his weekly piano lesson at his teacher's apartment. Lots of children in Germany learn musical instruments.

Monday, January 17

Scheffelstrasse 84
3rd floor
71903 Freiburg
Germany

Hi Kerry,

I'm glad the potato pancake recipe worked. It's delicious, isn't it? Today at school we had math, art, and gym. I love math. Our teacher, Frau Ernst, makes it really fun. She tells us a story and then gives us math questions. I always work them out quickly! I also love soccer. I play at recess and after school in a soccer club.

What's your school like? Write back and tell me.

Tschüss! (Pronounced "Choos." This means "Bye!")

Paul

In the math lesson, our teacher called out the number seven and we had to get into groups of seven.

Off to Work

Paul's dad is a doctor. He works in a hospital in Offenburg, a city 35 miles (60 km) away from Freiburg. He takes the train there every day. Paul's mom is a physiotherapist. She helps children to learn to move their bodies properly. She drives to work at a nursery.

Here is Paul's mom at work, helping a girl to improve her balance.

This scientist is doing medical research in a laboratory at the University of Freiburg.

Many people in Freiburg work in modern industries such as IT, biotechnology, and solar industries. Many others work in service industries, for example, running Freiburg's great transportation system.

In the countryside around Freiburg, there are many jobs in vineyards, picking grapes and making wine.

Free Time

Germans have up to six weeks' vacation every year, as well as weekends off. People spend their free time at sports centers, theaters, movie theaters, libraries, or campsites.

Soccer is the most popular sport. Most Germans belong to a sports club or other type of club to do their favorite pastime.

Paul is the goalie in his soccer team. Here he is playing in a school tournament. His team won third place.

There are four indoor pools and three outdoor pools in Freiburg, as well as a learners' pool.

Paul loves soccer, biking, swimming, and reading. On weekends, the family goes to the park or swimming pool, or for a bike ride. In the summer, they often rent a house in Italy, France, or Switzerland and spend a few weeks there with friends.

Paul and his friends have turned a table upside down so they can play with their spinning toys.

Religion

Two thirds of the people in Germany are Christians. There are also about 3 million Muslims, and some Buddhists and Hindus. Nearly a third of the people do not follow any religion. The biggest Christian festivals are Christmas, Carnival (in February), Easter, and Pentecost.

Paul lights a candle in the cathedral and prays for a family friend who is sick.

This Muslim boy is praying at the mosque in the Islamic center in Freiburg.

Tuesday, February 8

Scheffelstrasse 84
3rd floor
71903 Freiburg
Germany

Hi Kerry,

It was amazing here last week because it was Carnival (we spell it *Karneval* in German). Carnival is a time for having fun before the serious time of Lent. On Thursday, we wore fancy dress and joined the crowds in the city center. There were food and drink stands everywhere, and people were dancing in the streets. All weekend there were celebrations. On Monday it was the final procession with carnival groups from all around Freiburg.

Do you have any carnivals?
Write back and tell me.

Tschüss!

Paul

Here I am with Carla —
we've dressed up in fancy
dress for Carnival.

Fact File

Flag: Black, red, and gold became Germany's national colors in the nineteenth century. Different flags were used in the early twentieth century. In 1949, West Germany adopted the flag below. After Germany became one again, this became the flag of the whole country.

Capital City: Berlin is the capital of Germany. When Germany was divided into two countries, Berlin was divided too. After Germany became one country again in 1990, Berlin became its capital.

Other Major Cities: Hamburg, Munich, Cologne, Frankfurt, and Essen.

Population: More than 82 million. Germany has the largest population in Europe.

Size: 137,239 square miles (57,021 km²).

Language: German.

Currency: The euro (€), which is divided into cents. There are 100 cents in a euro.

Famous Buildings: Germany has large Roman Catholic cathedrals, including the Dom in Cologne, the Münster in Freiburg (above), and the Frauenkirche in Munich. It is famous for its castles, especially the Royal Castles in the Bavarian mountains.

Main Religions: 68 percent of Germans are Christians. About 3.7 percent are Muslims. There are also Orthodox Christians, and some Hindus, Buddhists, and Jews. Around 28 percent of Germans do not practice any religion.

Main Industries: Iron, steel, coal, cement, chemicals, machinery, vehicles, electronics, food and drink, shipbuilding, textiles.

Famous People: Germany is famous for its composers, thinkers, and scientists from the past, such as the composer Johannes Brahms (1833–1897) and the scientist Albert Einstein (1879–1955). Adolf Hitler was Germany's brutal leader from 1933 to 1945. Marlene Dietrich (1901–1992) is the best-known German actress.

Highest Mountain: Zugspitze, 9,715 feet (2,962 m).

Longest River: The Rhine, 862 miles (1,390 km). The Rhine has many old and famous cities along its banks. There are also industrial cities that pollute the waters.

Stamps: Stamps in Germany show famous people from the past, important events, buildings, plants, and animals.

Glossary

biotechnology Using living cells for industrial and scientific work.

carnival A big festival in many Christian countries just before Lent, with music, dancing, and food.

cathedral The main church in an area.

Lent The season of forty days before Easter when Christians think about things they have done wrong.

medical research The study of ways to improve medicines.

Orthodox Christians Members of Eastern Churches, such as the Greek and Russian Church.

physiotherapist A person who teaches people exercises to strengthen their bodies.

plains A large area of flat ground.

service industries Businesses that serve people rather than making goods, such as hospitals, tourism, and transportation.

solar Using the sun's energy.

tournament A sports competition with different teams, which leave the competition when they lose. At the end, there is one winning team.

vineyard A piece of land where grapes are grown for making wine.

World War II A major war that was fought from 1939 to 1945. The United States, Russia, Britain, France, and other countries defeated Germany, Italy and Japan.

Further Information

Information books:

Foley, Ronan. *A River Journey: The Rhine*. Chicago: Raintree, 2003.

Hirst, Mike. *We Come From Germany*. London: Hodder & Stoughton Childrens Division, 2003.

Gower, Teri, Morris, Ting & Wright, Rachel. *Country Topics: Germany*. London: Franklin Watts, 2003.

Park, Ted. *Take Your Camera to Germany*. Chicago: Raintree, 2003.

Paul, Tessa. *Fiesta!: Germany*. London: Franklin Watts, 2001.

Pluckrose, Henry. *Picture a Country: Germany*. London: Franklin Watts, 2001.

Reynolds, Jeff. *Germany (A–Z)*. New York: Children's Press, 2004.

Roop, Peter. *A Visit to Germany*. Chicago: Heinemann, 1999.

Schanz, Sonja. *Changing Face of Germany*. Chicago: Raintree, 2002.

Townsend, Sue. *World of Recipes*. Chicago: Raintree, 2003.

Web sites:

German Culture
www.germanculture.com.ua/
Facts, history, recipes, and tips.

CIA Factbook
www.cia.gov/cia/publications/factbook/
Facts and figures about Germany and other countries.

Germany for Kids
www.germany-info.org/
Use the search engine on this site to find out all about home, school, music, food, free time, and religion

Songs in German
www.songsforteaching.com/germansongs.htm
Read the words and hear the music for some German songs.

Index